Ex-Imam Reveals the Real Islam

Christina Bardstrum
with Hypatia Angel

www.christinafortruth.com

Ex-Imam Reveals the Real Islam / Christina Bardstrum with Hypatia Angel —1st ed.
ISBN-13: 978-0-9966840-1-9

Contents

Introduction

A FEW YEARS AGO, because I had just returned home after living 15 years in an Islamic nation, I was introduced by a Kurdish friend, Hypatia Angel, to some books about the Qur'an and Islam. The author, she explained, a former imam (Islamic teacher) of 24 years, Arif Tekin, now lives in self-imposed exile because of his many books which expose the truth about Islam.

My Kurdish friend Hypatia, who had become a Christian through a series of events over her young life, began to explain to me how these books had helped open her eyes to the truth about Islam. At her urging, I took one home to have a look.

The next time I saw Hypatia she said, "We should translate one of these into English!" Thinking I had no time to translate a book by a Kurdish imam academician, I was not interested. I had barely scanned the book she had given me.

A few months later in a second-hand bookstore in Florida I picked up a very old book, the biography of Abdul Aziz Ibn Saud, called "Lord of Arabia." I bought it because I love old books - especially old books about the history of the Middle East.

I devoured the biography of Saud, because it made the pieces of history I'd read earlier on that part of the world fall more neatly into place. I looked again at the former imam's book from Hypatia and decided to dive in.

The translation alone was a two-and-a-half-year project. The author, Arif Tekin, is an academic and he writes for academics. It was like a research project for me; there were Arabic words (not the language of the writing) and names of cities and books and authors — all with which I was not familiar.

I worked on it alone, for the most part, for two years. Hypatia and I then went over the whole manuscript together, mostly on the phone late at night after her evening job, which was after her class work as a student in a masters program. At last, we finished a 312-page book in English.

Although I was grateful for the opportunity to have learned all I learned personally via the translation work, I knew the message of the book would not likely reach the average American reader in its current form and would need to take on a different guise. I worked on dissecting the 312 pages and footnotes to find the most important facts for Western readers.

The truth about women in Islam is but one topic skillfully and almost totally white-washed for Western consumption. Should most Westerners also know something on such topics as the suicidal tendencies of the "Prophet" after his supposed revelations from the angel Gabriel, the scandalous politics and murders surrounding the Qur'an's official appearance, and the extreme moral depravity of the founders of this religion, perhaps there would be less of a tendency for seduction by this "religion of peace."

I have quoted Mr. Tekin throughout, and included his references to the Islamic sources. I included these sources' names and details so that you, the reader, can see these actual references in which Muslims trust. This will give you confidence in what you know is the truth about Islam. Very little Islamic source material, other than the Qur'an, is available in anything but Arabic. If it were translated into English, it is doubtful the translation would not be tainted.

This isn't exactly pleasant material to read, but my hope is that I have made the information at least easy to decipher. We in the West need to know these things and have them in our mental arsenal.

It will be important, before you begin, to read the Glossary of Names and Terms in order to have a reference for the Arabic words.

My quotes from the Qur'an are taken from the translation by M.A.S. Abdel Haleem, Oxford University Press.

This book will supply you with facts about the following, direct from the Islamic sources' quotes:

- *The call for annihilation of Christians and Jews by the followers of Islam (Ch.7, 8, 9)*

- *America as a zone marked off for jihad (Ch.10)*

- *The impossibility, apart from a sovereign act of God, of a peace between Israel and Islamic peoples.(Ch.10)*

- *The legality of lying and treachery in Islam (Ch.10)*

- *The illegality in Islam of friendship with non-believers (Ch.10)*

- *Muhammad's child bride, his condoning of the possession of sex slaves and of wife-beating. (Ch.1)*

- *Early Islamic leaders' treatment of women, concubines and slaves (Ch.2)*

- *Qur'an verses which are identical to lines of poetry of Muhammad's day (Ch.3)*

- *The cover-up of Muhammad's literacy (Ch.4)*

- *How the Qur'an actually came into being - after Muhammad's death (Ch.5)*

- *The accepted belief that Allah "takes back" verses, and sometimes "causes one to forget" them (Ch.7)*

- *Violent murders by Muhammad of those who were not submissive, or who merely criticized him (Ch.8)*

- *Muhammad's hatred for and murder of Jews (Ch.9)*

I have also included clips from recent news reports which verify the continuation of these Islamic practices for fourteen hundred years.

- Christina Bardstrum

Who Is the Imam, Arif Tekin?

AN "IMAM" IS A religious teacher in Islam, a figure comparable to the local pastor.

I have met and spoken online several times with Mr. Tekin over the last three years while I've worked on his writings. He is, after a self-imposed exile, settled in his country of refuge — unfortunately far from his children and grandchildren. Describing himself to me as a "scientist", not a religious person now, he is one who enjoys his research into the roots of Islam because he hopes to bring this knowledge to many who are trapped by this religion.

Arif Tekin was born in 1954 in a village in southeastern Turkey near Diyarbakir. His mother tongue was Zazaja, a Kurdish dialect. Because there was no school in the village, his education began as a student of the Qur'an in the local mosque. I personally have travelled through many of these villages in southeastern Turkey and seen the village mosque/local school — almost always a very plain green concrete building with the minaret attached to it, donned with the old-fashioned megaphone apparatus on top for the call to prayer.

He worked to become proficient in Turkish so that he could have an elementary education. Without involvement in a formal school, he earned his elementary, middle, and high school diplomas by taking exams, and also became proficient in Arabic, since his schooling was at the mosque school, or the "madressa".

He was prevented from pursuing the further study he'd hoped for because of family responsibilities and his wife's ill health. It wasn't until 1994 that he graduated from the university called, The Ninth of September in Izmir, Turkey, which is, by the way, ancient Smyrna.

Mr. Tekin explained to me that he was one who didn't really understand the Qur'an, though he had studied in the mosque school for years. In his youth, he, like every other Muslim, believed that the Qur'an came from the Creator. After he began to comprehend the actual content of the Qur'an, around 1987, his doubts about its authorship surfaced.

He remained an imam until 1988, being obliged to stay in his profession because of his responsibilities as the father of five. He did not speak about his uncertainties, for fear of serious consequences. (To give an example, a contemporary of Mr. Tekin, Mr. Turan Dursun, was assassinated by two gunmen on September 4, 1990, outside his home in Istanbul. He had been a prolific writer and a critic of Islam).

Mr. Tekin says that when the time came to cut all ties with the Qur'an, he "no longer identified himself with even one sentence in its verses", and in fact had come to see it as mythology. Realizing also that there were many dangerous things written in its verses, he knew he had to gather the information that confirmed his new stance and write about it. He has since written fourteen books, published in Turkish, and is currently writing his fifteenth. Some of the titles of his books are *Roots of the Koran, Women in the Koran and Muhammad's Women, Unknown Aspects About Muhammad's Death, Muhammad's Trip to Outer Space,* and *Unknown Aspects of the Koran,* the book which Hypatia and I translated.

Islam Overview

ISLAM'S BEGINNINGS — *A Short Summary*

A simple introduction to Islam's basics could be described in the following outline:

The Two Recognized Periods of Islam's Beginnings, in Two Cities

1. Mecca

2. Medina

The Two Branches of Islam

1. Sunni

2. Shi'ah

The Trilogy of Islam's Holy Books

1. Qur'an

2. Hadith

3. Sira

Mecca Period —
The "Call" of Muhammad and His Lack of Success

Islam was founded by Muhammad its prophet, who was born in 570 AD into an upper class family in Mecca, Saudi Arabia. He was raised by an uncle after his father's death. He married in his twenties an older wealthy widow named Hatice, and began his spiritual pilgrimage by consulting Jewish teachers and Christian priests of various sects living around Mecca, and by frequent spiritual retreats into the mountains surrounding Mecca. When he was approximately forty years old he had his first encounter with a supernatural presence or personage whom he later declared was the angel Gabriel. It was shortly after this that he announced himself a prophet.

Arabia at this time was a conglomeration of tribes and clans. There were Jews in the north and a few Christian settlements. Constant tribal wars between the Arabs made survival in this part of the world a continual struggle. There were many reasons for the conflicts, but some were certainly due to religious differences. Most Arab peoples were polytheists.

Muhammad's tribe, the Quraysh, worshiped the moon god "Hubal". The figure of Hubal, in the shape of a human, resided in Kaaba, the famous shrine built around a venerated black stone, probably a fallen meteorite, in the city of Mecca. Kaaba housed not only Hubal, but approximately 360 other gods, along with images of Jesus and Mary.

Muhammad's announcement of his position as prophet yielded negligible results, about one hundred-fifty converts after preaching 13 years in Mecca. Things had to change, and they did — but it started with the ousting of Muhammad from Mecca.

Medina Period — Islam Catches On

The year when Muhammad was run out of Mecca and took his followers to Medina, a city about 100 miles north, became for Muslims the date of the beginning of Islam. The reason for this will be evident in the next paragraph. The year was 622 A.D., the year of the Hijra, or "the migration". Here is what happened.

Muhammad and his followers were impoverished after several months in Medina, so he began to send out raiders to steal from caravans of Meccans. There was money to be had from the sale of stolen goods and from ransom money for the captives they took. Suddenly the idea of this new faith began to take hold — there was loot for the adherents. Muhammad's followers were prospering, and their numbers increased.

Soon after this, Muhammad's modus operandi shifted from raids to war, and jihad was born — beginning at Mecca. First he openly attacked

Meccan armies to settle his score with the Arabs who had rejected him, then he attacked the Jews.

The history of Islam contained in the official biography of Muhammad and available in English, *"The Life Of Muhammad"* by Ibn Ishaq is helpful for anyone wanting to learn details of how Islam then spread throughout Arabia. Of course, as Mr. Tekin advised me once, "We don't know how much of it is true." At the same time, it is good to know how his life is perceived by Muslims, since this biography is part of their holy book trilogy. Other suggested reading is included on page 57 of this book.

In the first 130 years after Muhammad's death in 632 A.D., Islam's adherents conquered the entire Middle East, parts of North Africa and most of Central Asia, destroying classical Christianity and forcing all Jews, Christians or other religions to convert ("submit" is the meaning of the word "Islam"), or die. Muslims continued to conquer territory until parts of Europe and India fell, and on and on it went, and on and on it goes in the present day.

The Two Main Sects of Islam

Most readers are familiar with the terms "Shia" and "Sunni" Muslims. These are the two main sects in Islam. Essentially the differences are political, and stem from preference for, or the rejection of, one man whom many believed should have followed Muhammad as caliph. Those who follow "Ali", a relative of Muhammad and whom Shia Muslims believe was the rightful caliph after him, live mostly in Iran. These are the Shia Muslims. The other large population of Shia's live in Iraq, where they form the majority, outnumbering the Sunni's.

The rest of the Muslim world is Sunni, making up approximately 90% of all Muslims. Sunni means "those who follow Sunna", or Muhammad's words and deeds, not Ali. The Sunni's populate the majority of Saudi Arabia, Turkey, some of Iraq, and the rest of the Islamic lands. Though the Islam of the Shia government in Iran is totalitarian, oppressive and murderous to apostates, it is the Wahabi sect of Sunni Islam which originated and is still practiced in Saudi Arabia and which perpetrates the Islam we now see in groups like Islamic State, Hamas, Muslim Brotherhood, al-Qaeda, Hezbollah, Boko Haram, Salafi's and others. So in actuality, there is in both the two main sects of Islam what is called in the West, "radical" factions.

The Three-Part Holy Law of Islam

Besides the Qur'an, there are two other sources Muslim scholars claim as Islamic law: the Hadith, *(or Traditions)* of Muhammad, and the Sira, or biography of Muhammad. There are literally thousands of Hadith, or Traditions, which are the sayings of Muhammad and the things he did, which have been remembered by those who were around him. An interesting fact is that even Muslims question the authenticity of much of the Hadith, since many entries appear to have been written to sanction the views of political groups during Muhammad's time. The biography, or Sira, was written by Ibn Ishaq, a scholar who was born forty years after Muhammad's death, and who compiled his information from what he gathered from oral traditions.

Glossary of Names

Abubakr (or Ebubekir) (573-634 AD)
The second caliph (succeeded Muhammad), who was also Muhammad's father-in-law, officiated from 632-634.

Ali (the Honorable) (601-661 AD)
Cousin and son-in-law of Muhammad. According to Muslims of the Shia sect, he should have received the caliphate after Muhammad. In Shia Islam, Ali is, after the Prophet, the highest name.

Ayse (A'isha)
An important wife of Muhammad, his child-bride of six, whose marriage with him was consummated at age nine. She was a key player in the foundations of Islam, and to her many Traditions or Hadiths are attributed.

Buhari (Muhammad al-Bukhari) (810-870 A.D)
Wrote the Hadith or collection of sayings of Muhammad considered the most authoritative by Sunni Muslims. Bukhari was a Muslim scholar who lived one hundred years after the death of Muhammad.

Hatice (Khadija)
Most famous of Muhammad's wives, of the same tribe as Muhammad in Mecca, a wealthy businesswoman. According to some Sunni sources, she married Muhammad around age forty, while Muhammad was in his twenties.

Ibn-i Ishak (Ishaq) (died ca. 676 A.D.)
Author of the authoritative biography of Muhammad, a third part of *the Sira*.

Muhammad the Prophet (570-632 A.D.)
The founder of Islam, considered by Muslims the perfect model for humanity. He is referred to by Mustafa Ahmad Al-Zarqa, in his Hadith as "the very pattern of excellence, the noblest exemplar."

Muslim, ibn al-Hajjaj (817-874 A.D.)

(Historic figure, not the term for an adherent of Islam) He collected the Hadith of Sahih Muslim, which is considered by Sunni's to be the next in line to Buhari's in importance.

Osman (Uthman) (577-656 A.D.)

Fourth caliph, in whose reign (644-656) the official version of the Qur'an was brought forth. He was assassinated.

Al Taberi (Tabari) (839-923 A.D.)

Writer of some of the authoritative biographical work on Muhammad.

Umar (or Omer, Omar) (573-644 A.D.)

The third caliph, officiated from 634-644.

Zeyd b. Sabit (610-660 A.D.)

A Jew who was named head of the committee for the establishment of the Qur'an in its official form during the caliphate of Osman. He was involved in gathering the verses for the Qur'an from the time of the caliphate of Ebubekir.

Glossary of Terms

Caliph

The leader of the Islamic "umma" or community, in essence the papal figure of Islam worldwide. Muhammad was the first caliph.

Caliphate

The seat of government for Muslims worldwide. The last recognized caliphate, the Ottoman Caliphate, lasted around 500 years, ending in 1923 at the establishment of the Republic of Turkey.

The Hadith

"Traditions", one of the three sacred texts of Islam, composed of the things Muhammad said and did and which were recorded by numerous Muslims. There are hundreds of thousands of these, but there are two accepted as the most authoritative by Muslims: the Hadith of Bukhari and the Hadith of ibn al-Hajjaj Muslim.

Imam

A religious teacher of the Sunni sect. In Islam, he is the equivalent of the local pastor.

Kaaba (Ka'bah)

"The Cube", houses "the black stone", located in Mecca on site of the most sacred mosque. Muslims pray toward this cube, and those who make "haj" (pilgrimage to Mecca) encircle it a specific number of times.

Kafir

Non-believer, non-Muslim, "infidel".

Q.
In this book, abbreviation for Qur'an.

Qur'an (Koran)
The verses supposedly given by the angel Gabriel to Muhammad. It is one of the three sacred texts of Islam.

Republic
Within the quotes of the imam in this book, refers to the republic of his home country.

Sharia
Islamic law, which is based on the Qur'an, Sira, and Hadith.

Sira
Biographies of Muhammad, a part of the three sacred texts of Islam. These were written by Ibn Ishak and Al Tabari.

Sunna
A term signifying the collections of the things which Muhammad said and did.

Sura (Sure)
Denotes a chapter in the Qur'an.

Tradition
An official story or saying from Muhammad's life. "Tradition" is the English equivalent of Hadith. The traditions are part of the "Sunna".

Trilogy of Islam
The three books considered holy by Muslims, i.e. the Qur'an, the Sira, and the Hadith. The two which are not the Qur'an make up the "Sunna."

Year of the Migration (Hijra)
Refers to the year Muhammad migrated from Mecca to Medina, corresponds to 622 AD on the Gregorian calendar. This is considered by most Muslims as the beginning year of Islam.

Unquestionably, Christianity turned the world upside down because of the life of Jesus Christ. Muhammad the prophet, on the other hand, has been considered — both by his contemporaries and by Muslims ever since — as the perfect model of a human being and the one to be emulated in all ways and for always. Muhammad is to Muslims as Jesus Christ is to Christians. Therefore, if one wants to understand Islam, it is necessary to study the words of Muhammad and his life story, as well as the verses of the Qur'an.

CHAPTER ONE

MUHAMMAD AND WOMEN

IN THIS CHAPTER ARE details from Islamic sources of Muhammad's attitude toward women and his judgment of their worth — from marrying a six-year-old to legalizing and celebrating sex slaves.

1. The Murder of Women Does Not Incite Penalty

Muhammad's verdict on the penalty for the murder of women is that there is none. Here's what Mr. Tekin quotes from the accepted sources:

"A blind man had a concubine with whom he had produced two children. The woman, who didn't believe in the Honorable Muhammad, said many bad things about him. One evening as she was beginning to criticize him again, her husband started to beat her. He hit her with a metal object in her stomach and he killed her. When the incident was explained to the Honorable Muhammad, he said, 'Hey everybody! Witness this, because it was a woman, this man cannot receive any penalty whatsoever'." [1]

And another: *"The story that comes from the Honorable Ali, that, because a Jewish woman spoke badly about the Honorable Muhammad one of her extended family killed her, and the Honorable Muhammad did not enforce any penalty on the murderer."* [2]

1

And another: *"Caliph Ebubekir executed a woman during his caliphate for leaving the faith. Her name was Ummu Kurfe."* [3]

From AMNESTY INTERNATIONAL,
REVIEW OF 2017-2018, AFGHANISTAN:

VIOLENCE AGAINST WOMEN AND GIRLS

The Ministry of Women's Affairs of Afghanistan (MoWA) reported an increase in cases of gender-based violence against women, especially in areas under Taliban control.

In the first half of the year, the Afghanistan Independent Human Rights Commission reported thousands of cases of violence against women and girls across the country, including beatings, killings and acid attacks. Against the backdrop of impunity for such crimes and a failure to investigate, cases of violence against women remained grossly under-reported due to traditional practices, stigmatization and fear of the consequences for the victims.

---

2. Muhammad's Child Bride

According to the Hadith of Buhari. **Buhari 7,62,65:** *"Muhammad and Aisha were married when she was six. They consummated the marriage when she was nine. Hisham said, 'I was told that Aisha stayed with Muhammad from the age of nine until his death'."*

Things have not changed. In the second report below, our Nato ally, Turkey, further legalizes child marriages.

From the
NATIONAL COUNCIL OF RESISTANCE IN IRAN
in August 2018:

In 2016 there were 4,165 reported early marriages, that is marriages in which the bride is between 10-14 years of age. In Iran, a marriage may be lawfully performed by a Shia Sheik and not reported to the government, rendering this number most likely lower than the actual. The legal age for marriage since Sharia law was instated in Iran is: 9 for girls, 14 for boys.

Quoting an article from Gatestone Institute in March, 2019:

. . . As if all the above were not bad enough, the Turkish government has put a "repentance" bill" before the parliament that, if passed, will enable courts to "delay punishment or defer the announcement of a verdict" concerning men who marry underage girls.

The new bill, expected to be voted on ahead of the March 31 local elections, aims to lower the age at which sexual relations with a child (under the cover of marriage) is considered a crime from 15-years-old to 12-years-old. If it passes, it will "pardon" the underage-marriage offenses of approximately 10,000 men currently serving prison sentences on sexual-abuse charges.

3. The First Caliph of Islam and His Concubines and Slaves

According to Islamic belief, if a concubine's lord dies before she has born him a child and she becomes a widow, she then becomes the property of his heirs and they are granted rights to her. If those of the heirs agree among themselves to sell her, they can divide the money among themselves, or make some other agreement. In short, she is a piece of property.

Among the companions of Muhammad, one of the most important ones, even until his death, was a slave concubine. Mr. Tekin says, "While Muhammad was ill, he released forty of his slaves. Now, it is not asked, is it, why these were not released earlier, why they were still under his ownership?"[4]

In the Traditions, slaves must always be kept under tight control. Here's a quote cited by Mr. Tekin from the Hadith: *"If perchance a slave escapes from his/her lord he/she is an infidel. If she marries without the permission of her master, she is an adulteress. If a slave escapes from her master and takes refuge in a group of infidels, there is a multiple obligation."*[5]

From the **Hadith of Buhari:** *"When I saw the honorable Muhammad, he had two ladies at his side, Ebubekir, and five slaves."*[6]

4. Muhammad Condones Taking Women Captives for Sex Slaves

"We were going to a battle, and the Honorable Muhammad told us that we could have sexual relations with the foreign women." This example has been recorded in both **Buhari and Muslim**.[7]

Here is an example from Mr. Tekim of a story of a Muslim jihadist around the year 627. Remember, these are some of the "holy" writings of Islam. Quoting the Hadith:

*"We joined the Mustalik attack (this happened in the fifth year of the migration). In this attack we took some beautiful women. (The Honorable Muhammad chose Cuveyriye for himself, and everyone knew this.) Because we had been far from our women for a long time, sex made us crazy. So we agreed that when we had sex with them, in order that they would not become pregnant, we should do some prevention. So we said, 'Let us ask the Honorable Muhammad if this is permissible', and he answered us, 'If one human, in his destiny, has to come now and join the world, he will come. So you are free, whatever you want to do'." These things are recorded many times in **Buhari and Muslim**.*[8]

And another: *"During the takeover of Mecca, we stayed in Mecca fifteen days. The Honorable Muhammad gave us permission to have sexual relations with whichever women we wanted, with a verbal agreement between the man and woman and a little money. After that, when my friends and I saw a woman on the street, we offered her money and I took her. I continued with her until Muhammad prohibited it."* There are many examples like this.[9]

5. The Islamic Slave Trade Continued

It is estimated that the Arab slave trade has affected more than 17 million people for over 1300 years. Slavery was legitimized by Muslims. See in the following quotes from Muslim scholars of the 14th and 15th centuries racial superiority to an obscene degree, and a calloused lack of regard for other human beings:

THE TUNISIAN ARAB HISTORIAN, Ibn Khaldun (1332-1406) wrote "the only peoples to accept slavery are the Negroes, because of their lower degree of humanity, their place being closer to the animal stage." Ibn Haldoun, Al-Muqaddim, Prolégoménes, 1857.

THE ALGERIAN ARAB THEOLOGIAN Ahmed Al-Wancharisi (1430-1508): "I have been asked about slaves from the land of Abyssinia who profess monotheism and accept the rules of the Holy Law: is it legal or not to buy and sell them? ... If their conversion to Islam comes after the establishment of a property right (on these slaves), then Islam does not demand liberation, because slavery was caused by unbelief. The state of servitude persists after the disappearance of unbelief because of its existence in the past." Kitab al-Mi'yar al-Mughrib, in Bernard Lewis, Islam. Paris: Gallimard, Quarto, 2005.

But these practices continue:

From GATESTONE INSTITUTE December 20, 2015:

ISIS Selling Yazidi Women and Children in Turkey

Last month, after Kurdish forces recaptured the area from ISIS jihadists, mass graves, believed to contain the remains of Yazidi women, were discovered east of Sinjar. The German TV channels NDR and SWR declared on their website:

"IS [Islamic State] offers women and underage children in a kind of virtual slave market with for-sale photos. ... The transfer of money, as the reporter discovered, takes place through a liaison office in Turkey.

---

6. Other Quotes from the Qur'an on Women, Statements which the Honorable Muhammad Supposedly Received from the Angel Gabriel

Wives:

"Your wives are your fields, so go into your fields whichever way you like, and send ahead for yourselves. Be mindful of God: remember that you will meet Him. Give good news to the believers." **Qur'an, 2:223**

". . . If you fear high-mindedness from your wives, remind them, then ignore them in bed, then hit them. If they obey you, you have no right to act against them: God is most high and great." **Qur'an 4:34**

Inheritance Rights of Women:

"Concerning your children, God commands you that a son should have the equivalent share of two daughters." **Qur'an 4:11, also 4:176**

From AMNESTY INTERNATIONAL, 26 February 2019

HUMAN RIGHTS IN THE MIDDLE EAST AND NORTH AFRICA: REVIEW OF 2018, IRAN:

Dozens of women peacefully protesting against the abusive, discriminatory and degrading practice of forced hijab by taking off their head scarves in public were violently assaulted and arrested. Millions of others were routinely harassed and assaulted in public places by the "morality police" for failing to comply with Iran's strict Islamic dress code.

NOTES

1. Muhammed b. Ali el-Hanbeli, Muhtasar-u Sarimi-l Meslul, pg. 53. Ebu Davud, number: 4361, Nesai, 7/107, Darekutni 3/112, Hakim, 4/354, quoting from Beyhaki 7/60.

2. Buhari, Megazi, under the heading of the Honorable's illness, number: 4431. Muslim, number:1767.

3. Muhammed b. Ali el-Hanbeli, Muhtasar-u Sarimi-l Meslul, pg. 53. Ebu Davud, number: 4361, Nesai, 7/107, Darekutni 3/112, Hakim, 4/354, quoting from Beyhaki 7/60.

4. Ibn-i-l Cevzi, Ebu-l Ferec, el-Muntazam fi-l History, 4/33. The section on the death of the Honorable Muhammad.

5. Sunen-i Ebu Davud, number: 2078: Marriage, Slaves Who Marry without Permission of their Master section. Tirmizi, Nikah *(Marriage)*, number: 1111-12. Mugni, Ibn-i Kudame, 7/49, Marriage section. Ibn-i Ebi Seybe, Arranged Verses (Musannaf), Marriage section. Nesai, number: 3987.

6. Buhari, Menakib section.

7. Buhari, Nikah *(Marriage)*, 31, number: 5017-18. Muslim, Nikah mut'a section, number: 1405.

8. Buhari:

    1. Buyu *(Magic)*, 109, number: 2229.

    2. Itk, 13, number: 2542.

    3. Megazi, 32, number: 4238.

    4. Nikah *(Marriage)*, 96, number: 5210.

    5. Kader, 4, number: 6604.

    6. Tevhid, 18, number: 7409.

9. Muslim, Nikah, number: 1406.

CHAPTER TWO

OTHER EARLY LEADERS OF ISLAM AND THEIR WOMEN

IN THIS CHAPTER ARE details from Islamic sources on the character of Islam's founding fathers — men who were expert at examining, buying and selling concubines, and who unashamedly used women as mistresses.

1. Caliph Ebubekir: Brutal Execution of A Woman for Criticizing Muhammad

Mr. Tekin quotes the Hadith:

> "He (Caliph Ebubekir) appointed a certain Muhacir b. Ebi Umeyye to the office of governor of Yemen. The governor learned that a woman had cursed the Honorable Muhammad. In the end, not only were her hands cut off, but her teeth were all extracted. When Ebubekir learned of it he said it was good that the penalty had been executed, or else he himself would have killed her." [10]

And here is an example of an incident in the U.S.A. in 2009, by a Muslim man who owned a TV network:

ASSOCIATED PRESS: updated 2/17/2009 7:56:51 PM ET

<u>*ORCHARD PARK, N.Y.*</u> *– The crime drips with brutal irony: a woman decapitated, allegedly by her estranged husband, in the offices of the television network the couple founded with the hope of countering Muslim stereotypes.*

Muzzammil "Mo" Hassan is accused of beheading his wife last week, days after she filed for divorce. Authorities have not discussed the role religion or culture might have played, but the slaying gave rise to speculation that it was the sort of "honor killing" more common in countries half a world away, including the couple's native Pakistan.

http://www.nbcnews.com/id/29245206/ns/us_news-crime_and_courts/t/man-accused-beheading-wife-called-gentle/#.XR1W7S2ZOi7

---

2. Caliph Omer's Thorough Examination of Concubines Before Purchase

Here are a few Traditions about Umar *("Omer", "Omar")*: *"The substance of it is that one day Umar was looking at a concubine to purchase and he took her dress down to look at her. Later one of his sons said to him, 'Father, grant her to me.' Umar answers, 'She's not legal for you'."* This was because Umar had already seen exactly what he wanted, so he said she wasn't legal for him.[11]

"There are even more interesting examples", says Mr. Tekin. "During the Honorable Muhammad's time, concubines were taken to the bazaar, and the ones who sold them were given the title, *'Nehhas'*.[12] One day when they were there and looking at a concubine, and when they were turning her to the left and the right, Umar's son came. Immediately he approached the concubine and began to feel her, asking the whereabouts of her owner. *Actually when this man wanted to buy a concubine, he felt her hips and her legs.* Sometimes he pulled up her dress and looked directly at her hips, and would say that there was no problem handling a concubine. He would say something like, *'Handling a concubine is no different than handling a wall'."*

From a book of another Tradition scholar, A. Rezzak, Mr. Tekin cites a special section of several hideous Traditions about the incident of Umar's son feeling the concubine at the bazaar. *"Apparently he looked over every part of her except her genital organs, but many Traditions say he even handled those."*

According to Mr. Tekin, a scholar named Elbani, a popular Islamic thinker of the last years, when giving credence to these Traditions, affirmed the view that they are authentic and true. So it remains that in this matter, in the Honorable Muhammad's Traditions, *"When a concubine is being bought, the customer may look at her every area, only the area where he finds what he wants is forbidden."* [13]

From AMNESTY INTERNATIONAL, AFGHANISTAN Report 2017-2018:

"In August, a woman named Azadeh was shot dead by Taliban members in Jawzjan province. According to the governor's spokesman, the woman had fled some months earlier to a safe house in Sheberghan city due to domestic violence. She returned after local mediation, but was then dragged from her house and shot by Taliban members."

---

3. The Concubines of Zeyd b. Sabit, Head of the Committee for Establishing the Qur'an

Mr. Tekin writes that Zeyd's son, Harice, reports that Zeyd had an Iranian concubine. So that she wouldn't become pregnant he used protective measures, but then she became pregnant anyway, in spite of this. He then said the child was not his, enforced the punishment of an adulteress on her, and instructed her to release the child. Of course, even if the concubine is penalized as an adulteress, her duties as a concubine continue. This is the incident. However, a different telling of this exists, and it is this: Zeyd asks the woman whose child it is. The woman replies that it is his. Zeyd answers her, "You are lying. I don't want a child from you; I am only using you as a mistress."

Mr. Tekin continues: "It remains then, that, along with Omer, we have Zeyd's doings, and from the Islamic sources we learn that these are their life stories — but they will not be told in the Qur'an! According to historians like Zehebi and Ibn-i Sa'd, Mr. Zeyd was husband to four wives and had 28 children!"[14]

The lifestyles of the founders of Islam were as per their prophet.

Disturbing news from a Newsweek, 6/8/17 article by Janice Williams:

More than 200 million women and girls in over 30 countries have undergone female genital mutilation procedures, according to the World Health Organization, and some 3 million girls are estimated to be at risk of being subjected to the procedure, which can include partial or total removal of genitalia in an effort to suppress female sexuality.

While the procedure is more common in countries in Africa, the Middle East and Asia than in the U.S., a physician has recently been accused of cutting up to 100 girls in a doctor's office in Michigan.

https://www.newsweek.com/
genital-mutilation-girls-michigan-doctor-623295

NOTES

10. Kadi Iyad, Sifa *(Healing)* 2/222 and following.

11. Imam Malik, Muvatta, marriage section, number: 1146. A. Rezzak, Musannaf, (Arranged Verses), 6/280, number: 10839-40.

12. Ibn-i Ebi Seybe, Musannaf (Arranged Verses), Magic, 29, Vol. 7/185, number: 20492, footnote.

13. a. Abdurrezzak, Arranged Verses, 7/285, number: 13198-13209.

    b. Ibn-i Ebi Seybe, Arranged Verses, Magic, number: 20492-20499, section 29, Vol. 7/185 and following.

    c. Elbani, Igva-ul Galil, 6/201, number: 1792.

    d. Beyhaki, Sunen-i Kubra, Transactions chapter, 5/537, section 69, Tradition number: 10789-90.

14. Zehebi, Siyer-i A'lem, Zeyd b. Sabit material, number: 85, 2/428. Women and children:

    a. Of the lady Cemile binti Sa'd bin Rebi would be these children:
       1) Sait 2) Harice 3) Suleyman 4) Yahya 5) Amare 6) Ismail 7) Esat 8) Ubade 9) Ishak 10) Hasene 11) Amre 12) Umm-u Ishak 13) Umm-u Gulsum

    b. Of the lady named Amre b. Muaz b. Enes these children:
       1) Ibrahim 2) Muhammed 3) A. Rahman 4) Ummu Hasan

    c. To Ummu Veled (a war concubine) these were born:
       1) Zeyd 2) A. Rahman 3) Ubeydullah 4) Umm-u Gulsum

    d. Others of Ummu-l Veled (the same war concubine):
       1) Salit 2) Imran 3) Haris 4) Sabit 5) Safiye 6) Karibe 7) Umm-u Muhammed

CHAPTER THREE

MUHAMMAD'S RECEIVED VERSES

— WERE THEY FROM GABRIEL? OR NESTORIAN PRIESTS, ARAB POETS, AND FOREIGN SLAVES?

IN THIS CHAPTER ARE quotes from the sources to verify that many of the Qur'an verses match up to poetry of the day, that people of Muhammad's day were suspicious that his visits with foreign priests and slaves provided his "revelations", and that his experience of the angel "cleansing his heart in the waters of the brook Zemzem" is the same experience written about by a poet of his day who had died in the ninth year of the migration.

Let's consider some of the stories concerning Muhammad's beginnings as a prophet and his influencers. These are from the Mecca period before he was widely known as a prophet.

1. The Nestorian Priest, Varaka

First of all, there was the cousin of Hatice *(Muhammad's older wife)* named Varaka *(or Waraqah)*, who was a Christian priest, supposedly of the Nestorian sect. Notice in the quote following that the words of a poem read by Varaka appear later in Qur'an verses!

Quoting Mr. Tekin: "He *(Varaka)* was a knowledgable scholar on several religions. According to Islamic sources, when Muhammad returned the first time from Hira Mountain and he was explaining the things *(revelations)* he saw, he told Hatice and she communicated to Varaka. Varaka said, 'Ah, what can I do? If my life could continue I would be a helper to Muhammad. The signs show that he is a prophet'. Then he apparently read a long poem eulogizing and praising Muhammad. From these poems, close to forty verses of the Qur'an came, as per the source of Ibn-i Kesir.[15] It is not known who actually composed these poems or when they were written."

The most interesting thing about Varaka, however, is that, after his death, Muhammad's revelations ceased. In the quote below, Mr. Tekin seems to infer that Muhammad had relied heavily on Varaka for his revelations.

"From **Buhari** and also from some others, especially from the "Tabir" chapter *(of Buhari's Tradition)*, an interesting notice was given: *'When the Christian Varaka died, Muhammad no longer received revelation. He was very grieved over this'.* This ending or cutting off of the revelations was generally accepted by the Muslim people, but there is much dispute on this matter."

Mr. Tekin continues: "There are verses about this lack of revelation. The controversy is opened from the first of the **Al-Duha** *(translated, "The Morning Brightness", Q. 93)* chapter of the Qur'an. For us here, it's not so important about the length of the controversy over the ending of the revelations. The important thing is the fact that apparently, the God who gave these messages stopped them after the death of Varaka. Because of all this, Muhammad many times went to the mountain to attempt suicide, but Gabriel apparently came every time and calmed him and caused him to quit thinking about it. This is explained plainly."

Mr. Tekin asks: "Why did this God stop the revelations, after which on many occasions there was mockery by non-believers who said harsh things, such as suggesting that his relationship had been with Satan and that Satan had cut it off? The important thing to note is that the stopping of the revelations coincided with Varaka's death."[16]

2. Influences of Foreign Slaves

At this time, while Varaka was alive, the threesome of Muhammad, Hatice and Varaka studied various writings of other religions and languages and even some documents discovered in the Kaaba, apparently discussing among themselves what should be done with this knowledge.

Notice in the quote below how that, after it was known that Muhammad visited often with these foreigners, and afterwards, when there were objections from the people who began to disbelieve his revelations, suddenly "a verse came" which straightened out all this wrong thinking.

Quoting Mr. Tekin: "During Varaka's time, he *(Varaka)*, Hatice and Muhammad began to combine the knowledge which they had all gleaned from different sources. For instance, the three slaves of Hadremi's sons (Yesar, Yais, and Cebr) were also mentioned. They spoke different languages, and the Honorable Muhammad often went to see them and they came to him. His opponents, therefore, began to say as a criticism, 'Look, Muhammad gets his information from people, and then he says he is a prophet.' For this reason, in the **Al-Nahl** *("The Bee", Q.16)* chapter, verse 103, which came out afterwards, it says that the ones who supposedly gave Muhammad this information actually did not speak Arabic (and therefore Muhammad would not have learned anything from them!).

"This is the question: Since Muhammad could not read or write and their language was foreign to him, why did he come and go with them? For nothing? It is not debatable here that Muhammad often visited them because the people said that Muhammad had received his knowledge from people (*intimating they knew of these visits*). And also, since their language was foreign, did they live in Mecca like deaf-mutes?"

In other words, according to Mr. Tekin, those around Muhammad knew that he was visiting with foreigners — slaves, some from Yemen, priests, etc — and so they accused him of lying about where his revelations were coming from. It was then that the verse "appeared" in the Qur'an where Allah says that those who say Muhammad's teachings are from man are known to Allah, and Allah assures them that those with whom Muhammad is speaking do not even speak an intelligible language (and so could not possibly be giving him these verses which are in Arabic).

3. Poets of the Day and Muhammad's "Heart Cleansing"

The Qur'an contains amazing similarities to, and even the exact wording, of some poetry of Muhammad's day. One of the quotes of Mr. Tekin's below tells the story of the cleansing of Muhammad's heart after it was removed.

Mr. Tekin: "Actually, if the Qur'an were compared to the poetry of that day the conclusion would be surprising. The Qur'an is especially close to the content of the poetry of Umeyye b. Ebi Salt and Kuss b. Saide el-Iyadi. It is obvious that a very important source for the Prophet was earlier poetry — from before Islam."

Mr. Tekin on the Poet Umeyye b. Ebi Sait:

"I want to offer some information about one of this period's famous poets, Umeyye b. Ebi Salt. This man lived in the Honorable Muhammad's time; he was a famous poet and a learned man. According to some, he died after the second year of the Bedir War, others say he died in Taif (*a city in Mecca*) in the ninth year of the migration. This man knew much about Judaism, Christianity and the Hanif religions. He had done similarly to Muhammad in that he, like Muhammad, had gone to Damascus and become acquainted with priests.

"One day the Honorable Muhammad talked with Umeyye's sister about him. He asked her if she knew any of her older brother's poetry, and the woman began to give some information about him. She explained how, when he was sleeping, his abdomen was opened up and his heart was taken out and then put back into place.

"Now, as is known, the same kind of experience happened in the Honorable Muhammad's life! Before the ascension event, three angels came down, opened up his abdomen, took out his heart, and with water from the sacred well, Zemzem, washed it. Another person, speaking of this one called Umeyye had said the same thing, that his heart had been removed and washed. Actually, Umeyye had said to his friends that he put it back in place and then ascended to heaven. This story was first relayed in the writings of **Buhari** and **Muslim**."[17]

Again from Mr. Tekin, on the poet Kuss b. Said el-Iyadi:

"One day, a deputation from the clan connected to the poet Kuss bin Saide came to the Honorable Muhammad. He asked them, 'What happened to Kuss b. Saide?' They told him he had died. Muhammad began to share with them a memory of the poet: 'One day I saw him in a fair in Mecca, called Ukaz, where poetry contests were held. He was on a red camel, addressing the people fervently; it was an interesting talk. I'll never forget what he said that day.'"

Mr. Tekin's comparison of Kuss poetry with some of the sentences in verses in the Qur'an:

"When Kuss introduces God, *'We have a God like this; he created man and woman.'* In the **Al-Layl** *("The Night", Q.92)* chapter, the third verse, there is a similar sentence.

Also, this sentence, *'Every living thing will taste death'*, is used by Kuss in the open market talk we referred to, and this matter also is similarly mentioned in a few places in the Qur'an.[18]

When Kuss discusses mountains in his talk, he says, *'To ensure that the world would not wobble, the mountains serve as a kind of post, or pile.'*, an idea found repeatedly in the Qur'an."

According to Mr. Tekin, Kuss the poet was a Christian, but he was on the brink of a new religion in which he could call himself a prophet. To say, "I am a prophet" was common in the culture of that time. The one who promoted himself successfully was usually the one who got away with it!

At the time when Muhammad was doing his research, there were others named Museyleme and Tuleyha who were announcing themselves as prophets, and so Muhammad needed material. Poets like Kuss, Umeyye, and Imr-ul Kays became important sources of inspiration for him, and then when he came forth as the prophet of Islam, many of the verses he supposedly received in Mecca were identical with the lines of Kuss![19]

NOTES

15. El-Bidaye ve'l Nihaye, 2/362, and continuing. Hatice's Varaka b. Nevfel chapter.

16. 1) Buhari: a) Bedu-l Vahy, 3. b) Ehadis-i Enbiy, 21, number: 3392. c) Commentary, Alak chapter, verse 1, number: 4953. d) Tabir-l, number: 6982, this last tradition being very important.

    2) Muslim, Imam, 160. Also in the Story, History, and Tablets books there is detailed information.

17. Luves, Seyho, Suarau-l nesraniyye kable-l Islam, pg. 226.

18. Al-Anbiya *(The Prophets)*, 35 (Qur'an 21:35)

19. The workings of the poems of Kuss b. Saide are found in these chapters *(of the Qur'an)* which are all from the Mecca period: Hijr *(English name unknown)* Kahf *(The Cave)*, Maryam *(Mary)*, Ta Ha *(English Unknown)*, Anbiya *(The Prophets)*, Furqan *(The Differentiator)*, Shu'ara *(The Poets)* Mu'minun *(The Believers)*, Shura *(Consultation)*, Tur *(The Mountain)*, Najm *(The Star)*, Rahman *(The Lord of Mercy)*, Mulk *(Control)*, Muddessir *(English Unknown)*, Naba *(The Announcement)*, and Buruj *(The Towering Constellations)*.

CHAPTER FOUR

WAS MUHAMMAD ILLITERATE?

THE AGENDA OF THE WRITERS AND FOUNDERS

IN THIS CHAPTER, YOU will find proof from the Islamic sources that Muhammad was indeed literate.

Mr. Tekin addresses the question of Muhammad's supposed illiteracy by pointing out that it would have been unlikely for an illiterate person to conceive of something like receiving "verses", since such a person would not know of such things. The Qur'an verse used to later defend the supposed illiteracy of Muhammad is found in the 29th chapter, **Al-Ankabut** *("The Spider"),* verse 48: *"You, before this neither read a book nor wrote."* Mr. Tekin shows that the intent of this "neither read nor wrote" was most likely to put forth the idea that Muhammad was not a professional prophet before, nor was he in the line of prophets, or a "son of a prophet." The statement, instead of addressing his reading or writing abilities, was most likely meant to emphasize his unique position as a prophet in his own right.

1. The Probable Reasons for the Illiteracy Claims:

Mr. Tekin says, "The Islamic sources show that the Honorable Muhammad was a perceptive individual. The story was told that he was illiterate because if he had been registered as one knowing letters, people would have said that this book did not come from God. But let me point out that Moses, who grew up in Pharaoh's palace and was learned, also said: "I am a prophet." Being literate did not cast a shadow on his being a prophet. The followers of Islam seem to have put illiteracy on Muhammad to claim that a miracle had happened. This really is a shame, because it is not substantiated."

2. Quoting Mr. Tekin on Muhammad's Upbringing, his Employment in Business and his Literate Wives:

"The Honorable Muhammad was a clever child of a leading family in Mecca. So, how is it that his wives — the daughter of Omer, Hafsa, and the daughter of Ebubekir, Ayse — were literate, and yet Muhammad had not learned to read or write? How could it be that a child of a family in a position of government in whatever place one might live could remain ignorant? His uncle and guardian Ebu Talip looked after him well, and protected him and loved him very much. Many times he took Muhammad with him to Syria to trade in the markets. Why would one like his uncle, who loved him so much, leave him ignorant?

"Again, the Honorable Hatice took *(Muhammad)* as her chief employee and sent him to Damascus to do business with her enormous assets. If this man did not know how to keep accounts and didn't even know how to write, would Hatice have trusted him with her possessions? At that time, the term prophet was not attributed to him, such that Hatice should trust him because of this. He was only between twenty and twenty-three years old! Hatice's assets were greater than the assets of all the people in Mecca.[20] From this, we can understand that certainly Hatice chose a very good employee who knew how to write and was an expert in trading and account keeping. In essence, these circumstances deny any claims of the Honorable Muhammad being unable to write.

"Let me repeat: It is an unbelievable assumption that Muhammad would not be literate, given the fact that his wives, the Honorable Ayse, Hafsa, and Ummu Seleme had learned to read and write. His other women, i.e., Ukbe's daughter Ummu Gulsum, Sifa binti Abdillah Adeviye, Sa'd's daughter Ayse, and Mikdad's daughter Kerime were also literate."[21]

3. According to the Traditions, the Honorable Muhammad was Literate:

In the following three quotes, Mr. Tekin shows by the Hadith that Muhammad could write.

"When the Honorable Muhammad was on his death bed, he asked of someone, 'Bring me paper and pen, let me write my will.' At that time, Omer came and said that Muhammad was so ill that he didn't know what he was saying, and anything he would say in his condition would be invalid. And so the Honorable Muhammad didn't write that last will and testament. This Tradition, containing the name of Omer himself and his objection, is repeated three places in **Buhari**. It is also found in **Muslim**.

"The message I want to give you here is that the Honorable Muhammad said, *'Bring me pen and paper. I want to write you some important things.'* Muhammad even wrote a book about dues and duties; and these things are explained in the trusted Traditions.[22]

"In the Hadiths of both **Buhari** and **Muslim,** there is a Tradition that the Honorable Muhammad wrote a letter to the Greek emperor and to the Iranian Shah."[23]

In another instance, Muhammad sent a letter to the head of the company which he sent out to make raids, saying, *"If you should come to such and such a place, it should be opened."* Here is Muhammad himself writing a secret letter! In a quote from **Buhari** about this, offered by Mr. Tekin: "The Honorable Muhammad gives the letter he has written to the man, saying, *'Take this and give it to the prince of Bahrain.'* When the prince takes it, he sends it to the Shah, and then the letter is torn up. Here are two examples of the Honorable Muhammad's writing."[24]

4. On Muhammad's Reading Skills:

In another Tradition, there is the story of one of Muhammad's "competitor" prophets sending him a letter through a courier. When Muhammad receives the letter, he reads it and then asks if the courier believes this other "prophet". When the courier says he does, Muhammad replies, *'It's not customary to kill the ones sent, or else I would have cut your heads off.'* [25]

AMNESTY INTERNATIONAL,
IRAN Report 2017-2018:

The death penalty was maintained for vaguely worded offenses such as "insulting the Prophet", "enmity against God" and "spreading corruption on earth".

In August, spiritual teacher and prisoner of conscience Mohammad Ali Taheri was sentenced to death for the second time for "spreading corruption on earth" through establishing the spiritual group Erfan-e Halgheh; in October the Supreme Court quashed the death sentence. He remained in solitary confinement.

NOTES

20. Abdurrezzak Nevfel, Muhammed the Prophet, pg. 97.

21. Belazuri, Futuh-ul Buldan, pg. 661

22. a. Ebu Davud, Zekat *(Alms)*, 5, number: 1568-70.

    b. Tirmizi, Zekat *(Alms)* 4, number: 621.

    c. Ibn-i Mace, Zekat *(Alms)* 9, number: 1798

23. a) Buhari, Jihad, 101, number: 2939, again Jihad, 102, number 2940.
    b) Muslim, Jihad,75, number: 1774, Libas 13, number: 2092.

24. Buhari
    a. Ilim *(Wisdom)* 7, number: 64

    b. Jihad 101, number: 2939.

    c. Megazi 82, number: 4424.

25. Ebu Davud, Tribute 27, number: 3027, Abu Davud, Jihad 166, number: 2761.

CHAPTER FIVE

THE QUR'AN DIDN'T EXIST IN MUHAMMAD'S TIME

THOUGH IT'S USUALLY ASSUMED that there was a properly written book in the time of Muhammad called "The Qur'an", this simply isn't true. The information on the process of gathering together the sayings of Muhammad, which he claimed to be from Gabriel, is quite extensive. This work of "verse gathering" was done over several years and then put into a text called the Qur'an.

Mr. Tekin quotes a Hadith: "Actually, there were many Qur'an's, but in the Yemame War *(December, 632 AD, approximately six months after Muhammad's death)* many of the ones who had had the Qur'an memorized were killed, and so took many of the verses of the Qur'an with them. When Ebubekir, Omer, and Osman assembled the Qur'an, they did not find these, so they were lost. The failure to write the verses of the Qur'an became a disquieting thing."[26]

1. On the Beginnings of the Work on the Qur'an

Mr. Tekin says there are differing historical accounts as to how the Qur'an came into book form and why it was done.

"The Department of Religion in Turkey," Tekin says, "placed the Qur'an in the class of a writing which came in the form of an opinion, such as that of a reporter. This is interesting, because this means that this department is not persuaded that 'The Qur'an was brought together in the time of the Honorable Muhammad', no matter how many in Islamic works have said it. Heading up these accounts in the Islamic sources is the explanation in **Buhari**."[27]

"When he talked, like in our day, in the case of citizens listening to a governing authority, those who heard Muhammad and observed him perceived certain things. Then, after his death, the words of the Qur'an were taken from these perceptions and memories of speeches they had heard. Everyone who had received the Honorable Muhammad's words then began to shape the Qur'an verses and frame the sentences from the format he himself understood from all of them.

"Just as it is obligatory that a leader of an organization make a short declaration so that those around him, his disciples and followers, might put together a book or many books full of his words — in this way it happened after the Honorable Muhammad. Since it is a fact that the bringing together of the verses into a complete Qur'an spanned the period of two caliphates, one has to ask why all this labor was necessary if 'the Qur'an was brought together in the time of the Honorable Muhammad'."

2. Why the Verses Began to be Collected During Caliph Omer's Time

Quoting Mr. Tekin, "Some, according to the sources, say that the matter of putting the Qur'an into book form started first of all with Caliph Omer. One day he asked, 'On such and such a subject there is a verse. Who knows it?' Those around him answered, 'The one who knows that verse was killed in the war.'

"According to the work of Ibn-i Ebu Davud *(writer of some Traditions or Hadiths)*, Omer was called to the work, and it was announced that they were putting the Qur'an into book form and that those who had verses should come, together with two witnesses. The idea of gathering together the Qur'an verses came from Omer; there is no dispute about this. According to the Traditions, Omer continued to gather verses from the people who had two witnesses for each verse until he was murdered, leaving the work incomplete." [28]

So here you have the authoritative writing of the holy writ: those who could remember things Muhammad said, if they had a witness with them, came to the mosque gate and told Omer what they remembered.

3. The Second Stage of Qur'an Work During Caliph Osman's Time

Tekin writes, "In Caliph Osman's time, the second stage of the work was done. According to what is known, the work and the rationale of Ebubekir and Osman were different. For Ebubekir, it was most important that the Qur'an not be lost, and so he worked to assure it wouldn't be, but in a disorganized fashion. Osman, having in hand Ebubekir's prepared copy, brought out a new Qur'an and burned and destroyed all the copies that remained!" [29]

According to Mr. Tekin, the caliph Osman appointed four youths as his committee for bringing forth his new Qur'an. The following are some interesting details about the four.

1. Sait bin As: Sait was only nine years old at the death of the Honorable Muhammad. Of course, because he was a child, there is no direct Tradition from Muhammad! But there is a second-hand Tradition in the form of some quotes from the other companions. He apparently had not talked with Muhammad — of course, at that age, what kind of conversation could he have had? An interesting fact is that once the caliph Omer said to Sait: 'I won't apologize to you for killing your father. . . If he was your father, he was my uncle; we killed for religion.' [30]

2. Abdullah bin Zubeyr b. Avam: This man, who was later crucified, was the grandson of Caliph Ebubekir. When Muhammad died, the child was eight years old. His Arabic, like Sait's, was perfect. After Sufyan's son Yezit, he himself was chosen for caliph; later, the famous Hajjaj crucified him on a cross and murdered him without mercy. In six Traditions out of ten, Buhari tells this, in Salih Muslim two, and in every two Traditions in the sources, it is mentioned.

3. Zeyd b. Sabit: This person, the head of the committee, was originally from Medina. When Muhammad migrated to Medina, he was a child of eleven years old. In the third year of the Islamic calendar, the Uhud War broke out, but he, being only a child, did not join. This means that in Ebubekir's time when he had responsibility for the Qur'an work, he was a 20 to a 23-year-old guy. This is interesting, and another thing is that this man's father was a Jew.[31] According to historians, Zeyd was husband to four wives and had 28 children.[32]

4. Abdurrahman b. Haris b. Hisam: This man married Caliph Osman's daughter Meryem. The general opinion is that he was present, as a child, during Muhammad's life; this is counted as valid. He was wealthy. At his death, he had fifteen houses. It was evident he was Osman's son-in-law; he was also among the ones who were close to him and did well for himself.

NOTES

26. Muhammed A. Rauf el-Menavi, Faydul Kadir Serh-ul Mosque Sagir, 2/187, number: 1625-1626.

27. Buhari:

   1. Commentary, Tawba *(Repentance)* 20, number: 4679.

   2. Fedail-i Kur'an 3, number: 4986.

   3. Oracle Scribe section 4, number: 4989.

   4. Ahkam 37, number: 7191.

   5. Tevhid *("Monotheism")* 22, number: 7425.

28. a. Hindi, Kenz, number: 4759 Cem'ul Kur'an section.

   b. Suyuti, Itkan, 1/130, chapter 18.

   c. Ibn-i Kesir, Fedail-i Kur'an, pg. 59.

   d. Ibn-i Sa'd, Tabakat, Istihlaf-u Omer section, 3/157

   e. Ibn-i Ebu Davud, Book of Meshif, pg. 170.

29. Suyuti, imkan, chapter 18, 1/133.

30. Vahidi, Esbab-i Nuzul, Mujadala *(The Dispute)* chapter, last verse.

31. Ibn-i Sebbe, History of Medina 3/1008.

32. Zehebi, Siyer-i A'lem, Zeyd b. Sabit material, number: 85, 2/428.
Women and children:
a) Of the lady Cemile binti Sa'd bin Rebi would be these children:
1) Sait 2) Harice 3) Suleyman 4) Yahya 5) Amare 6) Ismail 7) Esat
8) Ubade 9) Ishak 10) Hasene 11) Amre 12) Umm-u Ishak
13) Umm-u Gulsum

b) Of the lady named Amre b. Muaz b. Enes these children:
1) Ibrahim 2) Muhammed 3) A. Rahman 4) Ummu Hasan

c) To Ummu Veled *(a war concubine)* these were born:
1) Zeyd 2) A. Rahman 3) Ubeydullah 4) Umm-u Gulsum

d) Others of Ummu-l Veled *(the war concubine)*:
1) Salit 2) Imran 3) Haris 4) Sabit 5) Safiye 6) Karibe
7) Umm-u Muhammed.

CHAPTER SIX

SCANDALS AND VANDALS AT THE QUR'AN'S APPEARANCE

IN THIS CHAPTER ARE the actual happenings around the bringing forth of the final authorized version of the Qur'an during Caliph Osman's reign (644-656 A.D.) These events took place no sooner than 12 years after Muhammad's death. My point in including this chapter is to show the crooked character of these founding fathers of the religion. The caliph's choice for manpower for the scholarly work reveals his character — i.e., his decisions were based on his political needs. This is part of the story. Other arresting details here are the events immediately surrounding the Qur'an's appearance. As you'll see, the people were terrified to speak anything against the caliph, understanding that he was putting out his own Qur'an as a power play. Those who opposed him finally found a way to execute him.

1. Those Chosen to Work on the Qur'an

According to Mr. Tekin, "From the beginning, from Mecca onward, there were many high-ranking companions with the Honorable Muhammad who were literate and who knew the Qur'an *(actually the verses which would become, at a later time, the Qur'an).* Then Osman comes in and establishes his committee with children like this and with his family members, and, according to the Sunni sources, Jewish Zeyd b. Sabit as the committee head!"

Mr. Tekin continues: "The subject of the ones who were the most knowledgeable of the Qur'an and how they were related to the matter of putting the Qur'an into book form is very important. Frankly, those who followed the Qur'an and were the most interested in it were not included in the committee at that time. These were people like Ubey b. Ka'b, Muaz b. Cebel, Abdullah b. Mesut, and Salim. Ibn-i Mesut had said that when he had seen seventy flaws in what Muhammad had given him, Muhammad replied with something like, 'Zeyd was not born of an infidel'." *(In other words, "don't cross me!")*

2. The Different Circulating Copies, Osman's Destruction of Them, His Murder

The existence of differing copies of the Qur'an during Osman's caliphate was discovered when Muslims from several regions fought against Armenians and Azeri's for control of Damascus. Those from Damascus preferred one version, Homs another, and Iraq two different versions — one for Basra and one for Kufa. Each claimed their own verses authoritative. Apparently, the arguments were heated, even between close associates.

Mr. Tekin says, "Ebubekir Abdullah b. Ebu Davud Sicistani gives in his book the names of twenty-six separate Qur'an copies and explains their differences.[34]

"In the end, the caliph Osman is said to have scolded the Muslims for their divisiveness on the accepted Qur'an: "What is this, one of you says Zeyd b. Sabit's Qur'an is correct, another Muaz b. Cebel's is right or Ubey b. Ka'b and the others are right! Were you with the Honorable Muhammad all those years and still this disagreement?" He then began

32

collecting the copies of the Qur'an done in Ebubekir's time and the one which was in the possession of Omer's daughter, Hafsa." [35]

The burning of the Qur'an copies by Osman is explained first in **Buhari**, but also in many of the Islamic sources. The fact is that when Osman was burning the copies, there was a huge controversy and the people were distressed — but no one spoke of it out of fear. In time, the Muslims' fears and their reactions to Osman became so intense that they killed him.

Quoting Mr. Tekin on the bad end to the bad story: "The events of Osman's burning of the Qur'an copies had a very negative effect among the people. At first, no one had the courage to speak out. It seems that some were accepting of the Qur'an he had assembled. Still there was harsh criticism, which resulted in a disturbance among the people of the community in the market and on the street such that it was said, 'It could be that one day Osman will be murdered.' And thus, Osman's end came."[36]

At this time, the Muslims who lived in Medina called back their friends in the faith who had been scattered to different geographical locations for the spread of Islam. Mr. Tekin offers a quote from the sources in which Muslims who had been summoned called for the murder of their caliph: *"Come back, you who moved far away to call those unbelievers to the faith! Come, because now the foundation is shaken! Come and let's declare jihad against Osman!"*

As the people became more and more enraged at him, Muslims from places like Egypt, Basra, and Kufa came to kill Osman. The main reason for this rebellion was Osman's burning of the copies of the Qur'an and insisting on his new one.

When the rebels finally took Ebubekir's son and used him to confront Osman, Ebubekir's son took him by the beard and held him in a room. Osman then asked, *"Why are you taking your revenge on me, my friend, Ebubekir's son?"* He mocked Osman, and finally said, *"You destroyed and burned the Qur'an — this is your crime!"* [37]

3. The Interesting Story of the Opposition of Abdullah bin Mesut to Osman's Qur'an and the Serious Consequences

Mr. Abdullah Mesut's story is telling. He was one who was with Muhammad from the beginning, migrated to Medina with him, and was recommended by the prophet for the organization of the verses of the Qur'an — but, as we've already seen, was not allowed. Mr. Tekin quotes **Buhari** who quotes Muhammad, *"Receive the Qur'an from Abdullah b. Mesut, from Huzeyfe's poor slave Salim, and from Ubey b. Ka'b and Muaz b. Cebel."* From these, Abdullah and Salim were from Mecca, and Muaz and Ubey b. Ka'b were from the Muslims of Medina. **Buhari** repeats this in a few places."[38]

Mr. Tekin also quotes **Buhari** on Mesut, *"In many ways Abdulla b. Mesut resembled the Honorable Muhammad."* So here you have Mr. Mesut, who was not chosen for the committee on the Qur'an, being recognized by the main Hadith writer, Buhari.[39]

In others' Traditions, it is written that Mesut often said he knew the Qur'an verses better than anyone living. It is also well known that Mesut and his mother went often to the home of Muhammad, and that Muhammad took care of Mesut and his mother as family.

Mesut was apparently at the head of the opposition when Osman's Qur'an came forth. Osman had given him a position in management and finance in the government in the city of Kufa, Iraq. At the same time, Osman had appointed the man named Velit b. Ukbe, a known enemy of Muhammad, one whom Muhammad had called an "evil person" and who was a known drunk, as governor of Kufa. This man came to Mesut one day to receive some provisions, which Mesut gave him, expecting to be repaid.

When after a time he was not repaid, Mesut went to ask for payment. The governor was irate and reported the incident to Osman, after which Osman reprimanded Mesut for demanding honest dealings from a government official.

Mesut resigned his government position in Iraq, showed up one day at the mosque while Osman was delivering an address, and was carried out later, his ribs having been broken by Osman's henchmen.

A quote from Mr. Tekin on the story of Mesut in the mosque that day: "When Osman was delivering a sermon one day in the mosque and Abdullah *(Mesut)* came in and he saw him, he had these words to say: 'Look here, now a nasty animal has come in. Whoever would eat with him will throw up or have diarrhea.' Ibn-i Mesut replied, 'I am a friend of the Honorable Muhammad, and I was with him in the Bedir War' (Osman did not join the Bedir War, and according to some stories he escaped it, which is why he was the subject of criticism here). Osman then gave instructions for his corrective penalty. His men grabbed his feet and he drooled on the ground. At that moment two of his ribs were broken, and it was two in the afternoon at that time, and the prayers were not made."[40]

NOTES

33. Buhari:

a. Fedail-i Ashab, section 26, number: 3758, Salim section.

b. Abdullah b. Mesut section, 27, number: 3760.

c. Menakib-i Ensar, Muaz b. Cebel chapter, 14, number: 3806.

d. Menakib-i Ensar, Uber b. Ka'b section, 16, number: 3808.

34. Sicistan, Mesahif, 1/153-386 explains these different copies of the Qur'an: 1) Caliph Omer's copy. 2) Qur'an of the Honorable Ali. 3) the copy of Ubey b. Ka'b. 4) the copy of Abdullah b. Mes'ut 5) Abdullah b. Abbas. 6) Abdullah b.Zubeyr. 7) Abdullah b. Amr. 8) the Honorable Ayse. 9) Hafsa. 10) Ummu Seleme. 11) Ubeyd b. Umeyr. 12) Ata b. Bir Rebah. 13) Ikrime mevla Ibn-i Abba.14) Mucahit b. Cebr. 15) Sait b. Cebir. 16) Esved b. Yezit. 17) Alkama b. Kays.18) Muhammed b. Ebi Musa. 19) Hitan b. Abdillah Reksai. 20) Salih b. Keysan. 21) Talha b. Musrif. 22) Suleyman b. Mehran/A'mes. 23) Caliph Osman. 24) Caliph Ebubekir. 25) Huzeyfe's slave Salim. 26) Ebu Zeyd.

35. 1. Buhari, Fedail-i Qu'ran, Cem'ul Qur'an section, 4, number: 4987.

2. Hindi, Kenz-ul Ummal, number: 4773 and 4775.

3. Bakillani's work named Nuket-ul Intisar, pg. 363.

4. Ibn-i Kesir, Fedaili Qur'an, pg. 78.

5. Ibn-i Ebu Davud Sicistani, Mesahif, Osman chapter.

6. Ibn-i Sebbe, History of Medina, pg. 992, Cem'ul Qur'an section.

7. Ebu Same Makdisi, entitled "el-Mursid'ul-Veciz", pg. 175.

36. a. Taberi, History, 3/333 and following.

b. Ibn-i Kesir, Bidaye, 7/222 and following.

c. Ibn-i Teymiye, Minhac-u Sunne, 3/206.

37. a. Ibn-i Asakir, History of Damascus, Vol. 39/403.

b. Ibn-i Kesir, Bidaye-Nihaye, 10/307. Events of the 35th Year of the Immigration, "Osman's Murderer" chapter.

38. a. Buhari, Fedail, 26, number: 3758, section 27, number: 3760. Menakib-i Esnar, section 14, number: 3806, and 16, number: 3808.

b. Muslim, Fedail, Abdullah b. Mesut section, number: 2462.

39. Buhari, Fedail, Ibn-i Mesut chapter, 27, number: 3763, and Megazi, 74, number: 4384.

40. History of Yakubi, 2/1

CHAPTER SEVEN

ALLAH "TAKES BACK" SOME VERSES

IN THIS CHAPTER, YOU will see that in the accepted Islamic sources, there is a theological case made for Allah sometimes "causing" verses to be taken back, or "forgotten", because they have become invalid! This concept is known as "nasih-mensuh" or "valid-invalid". This is the primary defense made by Muslims for the discrepancies in different parts of the Qur'an and also the other two parts of the Trilogy of Islam. I included this chapter to show the nature of the sheer madness of a faith whose "god" takes out verses he formerly put in and changes his mind like a fickle teenager!

It is general knowledge that the Qur'an verses which came in Mecca differ greatly from the verses which came later after Muhammad had immigrated to Medina. In the Mecca verses, for instance, there is tolerance of other religions, but in the verses from the Medina period, there is the command to perform jihad against kafirs.

1. Mr. Tekin Introduces the "Valid-Invalid" Verses of the Qur'an

"From the Honorable Muhammad on the subject: *Actually, with the coming of the Qur'an, the Old Testament and the New Testament became invalid, and it is because of this that the nasih-mensuh entered. On one day*

God came and gave a law, and later, the law He had sent He didn't accept, and so he sent another, so the Qur'an verse sent earlier was unacceptable'.

"There is also this, that generally both the verses validated *(nasih)* and the ones not validated *(mensuh)* stayed in the Qur'an: it is not well known which are valid and which are invalid. Actually, which are appropriate and which are not is according to the situation; the canon is elastic, and you can stretch it in any direction you want!

"In the Qur'an there are examples like this – both valid and invalid verses – that God took out. Neither appeared in the written Qur'an, however the valid ones are accepted as law. Following is a short illustration of this:

"Ayse said, 'In the first verse which came, if one child drinks the milk of a woman other than its mother or family ten times, he is counted as her child.' Then later, with the coming of another verse, this was dropped to five times, but until the death of Muhammad the Qur'an was recited as the first one quoted above. The truth is that there is neither ten nor five in the Qur'an; but many sect leaders took the five as the foundation. If neither were in writing, it seems that the one which was practiced became valid in the law which came later!"

According to Mr. Tekin, "This 'disappearing' is explained like this sometimes: 'In the Qur'an the verse isn't found, but it's apparent that it came and then was taken out again. Here, the second verse (nasih) is of no consequence, it doesn't matter.' There are written documents that a verse like this exists!"

Mr. Tekin continues: "Therefore, since, even though the verse was non-valid it stayed in the Qur'an, this makes it a meaningless thing we're talking about – and therefore many Islamic thinkers began to come up with something to defend this. One such defense is this: *'Even if it is invalid, it is Allah's words, and there is no harm in letting it remain included – nothing will happen.'* Also, *'If both the new and old stay, people will understand better the preciousness of Allah, and how merciful he is to them.'* With statements like these they gave value to the invalid verses!"[41]

38

Here are some real verses, quoted by Mr. Tekin, concerning the "disappearing and appearing":

1) *"If we erase one verse, or cause it to be forgotten, then we bring one that is better, or that is similar. Is not Allah's power sufficient for everything?"*

2) *"When we put one verse in place of another, it is that Allah, knowing what he causes to come, knows better. They say: 'You absolutely are a slanderer.' No, it's not like this. Most of these don't know anything."*

3) *"Allah erases what he wants and leaves what he wants. The source is with him."*

4) *"We will tell you, and you will never forget. You only forget according to what Allah wants."*

5) *"We swear that if we want to reveal verses, we certainly go and do it."* [42]

2. Concerning the Forgetfulness Which Is Caused by God

Quoting Mr. Tekin who quotes the famous **Imam Suyuti**: *"Concerning the verses of which this (valid-invalid) is meant, Allah, who sent the word has sometimes made it invalid. He sometimes replaced the words with others, or he removed the words from the people's minds and made them forget . . ."*

Here's an interesting reply by the prophet to two disciples about their memory work: *"Two people learned two chapters of the Qur'an from Muhammad. One day, they wanted to recite them when they were praying, but they couldn't remember them. They went to the Honorable Muhammad and told him 'We forgot it. Can you tell us again?' Muhammad answered them that God caused them to forget the chapter they were talking about."* [43]

3. Verses Which Are Different on the Same Subject:

On Religious Freedom

Mr. Tekin says, "There is religious freedom expressed in the chapters which came in the Mecca period, and then later in the Medina period, in the **Al-Tawba** chapter *(Repentence, Q.9)* the verse comes, saying, *"Unless it is a holy month, "kill the ones you find who are not Muslim".*[44] And then a third change came, *"Make war, until they agree to pay the jizre (the heavy tax)."*[45]

On the Length of the Fast of Ramadan

From Mr. Tekin, "Now let's move on to the verse about the fast. It says *'The Fast, as it was established from you all to the ones earlier, was written and obligatory',* (and then it continues, using the expression 'numbered days').[46] According to Arabic grammar, from the expression here of these 'numbered days', the obligatory fast was between three and nine days. This means the fast was not a month. The fast of one month to be observed during Ramadan is not found in the Qur'an at all! Concerning this number is the plural word, *'Eyyem/days'*. And the word *'Kille'*, since it is plural, and since beside it there is no figure or number found, the number must actually be between three and nine."

4. Mr. Tekin on the Addition of a Contradictory Verse to Justify Losses after war

"When the Muslims won the Bedir War, the Honorable Muhammad became lethargic, and at this time some interesting verses came about. Here is an example: *'I sent to you thousands of warring angels, and I will release fear into the hearts of the infidels, so strike their necks and cut off their fingers'.*[47] One year later when the Muslims were defeated in the Uhud war, Muhammad's uncle Hamza was killed, and Muhammad was wounded seriously (in addition, his tooth was broken). When the news came out, 'Muhammad was hit', a verse appeared: *'If a war is won, there are also losses.'* Now I'll give the translation of the same verse from the interpretation in the Department of Religion's Qur'an: *'If you (in Uhud) were wounded, without a doubt that group also (the idol worshippers and in Bedir) were wounded in the same way. We deal out such days among people in turn, for God to find out who truly believes, for Him to choose martyrs from among you.'*[48]

So we see from this that Allah sometimes strikes fear into the hearts of infidels in battle but sometimes deals out defeats to his people. This is all to find out who truly believes – but even better, so he can choose some martyrs for himself.

NOTES

41. Suyuti, Mu'terek, pg. 91. Zerkesi, Burhan, 1/353, chapter 34.

42. Baqara *(The Cow)*, 106, Nahl *(The Bee)*, 101, Ra'd *(Thunder)*, 39, A'la *(The Most High)*, 6-7, Isra' *(The Night Journey)*, 86.

43. Suyuti, (in his chapter), Baqara *(The Cow)* 106, Itkan, pg. 472, 47th chapter.

44. Tawba *(Repentance)* 5.

45. Tawba *(Repentance)*, 29. Suyuti, itakn, 47th chapter (Nasih and Mensuh), also Mu'terek, pg. 93.

46. Baqara *(The Cow)*, 183-4.

47. Al-'Imran *(The Family of 'Imran)*, 124-5 and Anfal *(Battle Gains)*, 9, 12, 17.

48. Al-i 'Imran *(The Family of 'Imran)*, 140.

CHAPTER EIGHT

EXTREME PENAL MEASURES IN ISLAM

MANY IN THE WEST believe the "radical" Islam we see today is not the true Islam, because Islam is a "religion of peace." In this chapter are quotes from their trusted sources describing extreme punitive actions taken by Muhammad, the "perfect exemplar of humanity" whom all Muslims are to emulate. These certainly knock down the claims of modern scholars that Muhammad merely meant an "inner struggle" when he spoke of jihad.

1. The Issue of the Cutting Off of Peoples' Arms and Legs

A very famous incident happened in the eighth year after the migration, or around 630 A.D. People from three different clans came to Medina to inform Muhammad that they had become Muslims. The weather in Medina didn't agree with them and they became ill. Muhammad then advised them to travel to a certain place about six miles from Medina to recover. The government provided them with camels. They then did as Muhammad had told them, including obeying his advice to drink the milk and the urine of the camels so that they would recover. They did, but then they killed the shepherd of the camels and stole the animals. These facts are recorded in the Islamic sources, including the name of the shepherd, the city where they were, and the clans.

Now Mr. Tekin's comments: "The topic's essential elucidation, which I've tried to explain, is in the Qur'an. Also, in the corpus of the Traditions, there is a very rich document. In short, no other topic in the Islamic sources has this much proof and proof that is so substantial. . . Also, from the past until today there is still among the Islamic authorities the 'my view' and 'your view' kind of thing."

Here is the Qur'an verse about this incident:

> *"The punishment of the ones who started the war against the Prophet and Allah should be that they are killed or hung, or their hands and feet tied together in a cross behind their backs and then cut off, or that they be sent into exile. This punishment is a disgrace in the world. In the hereafter there is a horrible torment also that awaits them."* **Al-Ma'ida** *("The Feast", Q.5:33).*

"Okay, so what really happened?", Mr. Tekin asks. "Let's look", he continues. "There are six principal Traditions in the sources which accept this as sound, and in a few places, there is more information about it. Let me especially mention the Department of Religion translation of the Tradition found in **Tecrid-i Sarih**: *'Early one morning, the Honorable Muhammad, having heard that the shepherd was killed and livestock was stolen, sent a group commanded by Kurz b. Cabir or Said b. Zeyd with weapons. In a short time the group found the people and brought them back to the Honorable Muhammad. At Muhammad's instruction their hands and feet were cut off and their eyes gouged out, and they were left there in a very hot place (in fact they left them to die). Of course they did die soon afterwards; but before that, those who carried out this sentence left this place in a fury, the place which was called the hottest place, "Harre". They had asked for water but they were not given it'.* "[49]

Take a look at the long list of references to this incident on Note 49 at the end of this chapter!

From AMNESTY INTERNATIONAL, 26 February 2019

HUMAN RIGHTS IN THE MIDDLE EAST AND NORTH AFRICA: REVIEW OF 2018, IRAN:

The Supreme Court imposed and upheld amputation sentences. In January, authorities amputated the hand of a man, referred to as A.Kh., in Mashhad, Razavi Khorasan province, reportedly for stealing livestock and other valuables.

2. Other Executions by Muhammad

Apparently, two writers of Traditions, Teymiye and Iyad, give hair-raising examples of those whom Muhammad had executed. One case was the decision to execute the two concubines of a man named Hatal, for reciting poetry against Muhammad. It seems, however, that one concubine escaped.

Mr. Tekin writes: "In the records of **Ibn-i Abbas** we have this: A woman named Esma criticized the Honorable Muhammad in poetry. In speech which would today be used by an artist, the woman expressed in poetry something disaffirming to him. *When Muhammad asked, 'Who will give her the necessary punishment of death?' one of her extended family answered 'I will do it', and immediately went and killed her.*"

There is another case that is famous because it involves one of the early experts on the Qur'an who was also Muhammad's first scribe, Ubey b. Ka'b. Both **Buhari** and **Muslim** cover this story in two chapters of the Traditions. Here's the quote: *"At the Honorable Muhammad's command, a* *person named Muhammad b. Mesleme with a few other Muslims murdered him.*"[50]. Mr. Tekin says that there are detailed explanations in the Islamic sources of the why and how of the murders of both Ka'b and another man, Ebu Rafi, both of whom were Jewish.

Mr. Tekin on Muhammad's executions of his criticizers: "For criticizing the Honorable Muhammad, Nad b. Harris was killed by the Honorable Ali. This penalty for criticism came into practice in the Mecca conquest and continued to be applied until Muhammad's death. This means it was not a passing thing; quite the opposite, until the Honorable Muhammad's death he himself applied it, deeming it totally necessary. [51]

"After the Mecca victory, in the tenth year of the migration, when the goods and gold which passed into the hands of the Honorable Muhammad during the Uzza raid were distributed to some, the words of those who objected were: 'You are giving more to those in authority and very little to the poor.' Muhammad instructed Ebubekir to kill the complainers. One man escaped." [52]

3. Incidents of Setting Victims on Fire

From Mr. Tekin, "In two places in **Buhari**, he quotes incidences of the Honorable Ali burning those who leave the faith. When **Ibn-i Abbas** heard this he said, *'These are true, and if I had been there I would have murdered them, because there is a tradition that those who leave the faith should be killed, though the Honorable Muhammad forbad burning with fire'*.[53] In the source of Imam Beyhaki, there are many instances recorded concerning setting people on fire. With these verses that I offered above, it isn't necessary to give an example or proof; these are the details. Certainly, they are not meant to be decorations; they are not there for nothing, and they don't just "light" on the Qur'an for nothing!"

NOTES

49. a) Buhari:

    1) Vudu 66, number: 233

    2) Zekat 68, number: 1501.

    3) Cihat *(Jihad)* 152, number: 3018.

    4) Megazi 36, number: 4192-93.

    5) Commentary, Ma'ida *(The Feast)* 33, verse 4, number: 4610.

    6) Tip 5, number: 5685, verse 6, number: 5686 and verse 29, number: 5727.

    7) Hudut 15, number: 6802, verse 16, number: 6803, verse 17, number: 6804, verse 18, number: 6805.

    8) Diyat 22, number: 6899.

    a. Muslim, Kesame, number: 1671.

    b. Ebu David, Hudud, number: 4364-71.

    c. Tirmizi, Taharet, Bab-u ma cae fi bevl-i ma yu kulu lahmuhu, number: 72-73.

    d. Ibn-i Mace, Hudut, number: 2578.

    e. Nesai, Tahrim-i Dem chapter, from the Tradition numbers 4020 to 4043, totaling more than twenty Traditions.

50. a) Buhari:

    1) Rehn 3, number: 2510.

    2) Cihat 158, number: 3031 and also 159, number: 3032.

    b) Muslim, Cihad *(Jihad)* chapter, Ka'b section, number: 1801.

51. Muhammed b. Ali el-Hanbeli, Muhtasar-u Sarimi'l Meslul, pg. 56 and following. Here there are many more sources given.

52. Muhammed b. Ali, Muhtasar-u Sarimi'l Meslul, pg. 75.

53. Buhari, Jihad 149, number: 3017 and Istitabet-ul mirteddin 2, number: 6922-23

CHAPTER NINE

MUHAMMAD AND THE JEWS

UNFORTUNATELY, MOST OF OUR knowledge about the relationship between Islam and the Jews comes from today's media coverage of the Palestinian-Israeli conflict. Obviously, much could be said here, but I will stifle the urge and simply point you to what Islamic law says about the Jews.

Muhammad, "the noblest exemplar" (Hadith, M. Ahmad Al-Zarqa) detested the Jews, as you'll realize from this chapter's references. These quotes should answer our questions about the vehement hatred for the Jewish people we see in Mr. Abbas in Gaza, and in Hamas, Al-Qaida, the Muslim Brotherhood and other followers of Sharia law, two of whom serve today in the Congress of the United States of America!

Jerusalem, never mentioned in the Qur'an, is sacred to Muslims because they have assumed that the place called "the furthest place of worship" in Qur'an 17:1 is the same as the area of Jerusalem called by Jews, "Temple Mount". From this spot, according to the Qur'an verse, Muhammad made his famous "Night Journey" to heaven! During Muslim control of the city in A.D. 705, Caliph al-Walid built Al-Aqsa, the mosque which stands on the Temple Mount today.

Sira , Ishaq 554:
"The apostle said, 'Kill any Jew that falls into your power'."

1. *The Murder and Captivity by Muhammad of the Last Jews in Medina*

In the following paragraphs, I quote Dr. Bill Warner, *Thirteen Lessons on Political Islam,* page 29. He is summarizing this particular incident in Medina recorded in the Sira, the officially recognized biography of Muhammad by Ibn-i Ishaq:

From Ishaq 684-693: *"That same day the angel Gabriel came to Mohammed at noon. He asked if Mohammed were through fighting? Gabriel said that he and the angels were going to attack the last Jewish tribe in Medina. Gabriel said, 'Allah commands you to go to the Jews. I am headed there now to shake their stronghold.'*

"So Mohammed called upon his troops and they entered to the forts of the Jews. Now the Jews of Medina lived in forts that were on the outskirts of Medina. Mohammed rode up to the forts and called out, 'You brothers of apes, has Allah disgraced you and brought His vengeance upon you?'

"Mohammed put the Jews under siege for twenty-five days. Finally, the Jews offered to submit their fate to a Muslim named Saed, with whom they had been an ally in the past. His judgment was simple. Kill all the men. Take their property and take the women and children as captives. Mohammed said, 'You have given the judgment of Allah.'

"The captives were taken into Medina. They dug trenches in the market place of Medina. It was a long day, but 800 Jews met their death that day. Mohammed and his twelve year old wife sat and watched the entire day and into the night. The Apostle of Allah had every male Jew killed by beheading.

"Mohammed took the property, wives and children of the Jews, and divided it up amongst the Muslims. Mohammed took his one fifth of the slaves and sent a Muslim with the female Jewish slaves to a nearby city where the women were sold for sex. Mohammed invested the money from the sale of the female slaves for horses and weapons.

"There was one last piece of spoils for Mohammed. The most beautiful Jewess was his slave for sex."

This can be read in its entirety in the English translation, *The Life of Muhammad, A Translation of Ibn Ishaq's Sirat Rasul Allah,* A. Guillaume, Oxford University Press, 1955. Whether or not the whole truth is told here in Mr. Ishaq's biography of Islam's prophet is unknown, but the important thing to remember is that this is the source believed by those who follow Islam, and therefore Muhammad, whom all Muslims are required to emulate.

2. Earlier Plundering of One Jewish Clan of Medina

Before the incident I just recorded, Muhammad had plundered the Jews of the Beni Qaynuqa clan in Medina for "breaking the treaty" that they had supposedly signed with him when he first came to Medina. This tribe were goldsmiths and lived in secure quarters in the city.

Muhammad gathered the tribe together in the market place and told them to convert, saying that his coming was in fact prophesied in their Scriptures (Q.2:159 states that the Jews had "hidden" the proofs and guidance which Allah had sent down and because of this he, "Allah", had rejected them). Finally, Muhammad besieged their quarters; they surrendered, and were exiled. Muhammad took all their wealth and goods. This incident can be found in **Ishaq 545-546.**

3. Allah Calls Jews "Apes"

In the following verse from the Qur'an, supposedly Allah is telling Muhammad that He had tested the Jews because they were not keeping the Sabbath, and He had given them time to change.

Quran 7:163-166: *"When they ignored the warning they were given, We saved those who forbade evil, and punished the wrongdoers severely because of their disobedience. When, in their arrogance, they persisted in doing what they had been forbidden to do, We said to them, 'Be like apes! Be outcasts!'"*

51

4. The Last Hour, When Trees Will Reveal the Whereabouts of Jews for Slaughter

This is a fairly famous passage from the Hadith of Sahih Muslim, in which Muhammad's hatred for Jews is clearly seen:

Sahih Muslim, Book 041, Number 6985: *"Abu Huraira reported Allah's Messenger (may peace be upon him) as saying, The last hour would not come unless the Muslims will fight against the Jews and the Muslims would kill them until the Jews would hide themselves behind a stone or a tree and a stone or a tree would say: 'Muslim, or the servant of Allah, there is a Jew behind me; come and kill him'; but the tree Gharqad would not say, for it is the tree of the Jews."*

Keep in mind that this is Islamic law and that Muhammad is "the very pattern of excellence, the noblest exemplar", according to the Hadith.

There is much, much more text in the Qur'an about the Jews as the enemies of Allah and all Muslims. Dr. Bill Warner, in his book quoted earlier in this chapter, says that 10.6% of the Qur'an verse content written in Medina, as far as literal word count is concerned, is anti-Semitic. He compares this to 6.8% in Hitler's *Mein Kampf*. It is interesting also to note that the words, "Mein Kampf", translate "My Struggle". The definition of Jihad is "struggle".

CHAPTER TEN

WAKE-UP CALL TO US AS AMERICANS

IN THIS CHAPTER, WITH the stating of five "whys", I hope to issue a wake-up call to us as Americans concerning the mandate issued first by Muhammad and confirmed over and over throughout Islam's history — the mandate to annihilate all who do not accept Allah and Muhammad.

Islam, a political system disguised as a religion, has, since the days of Muhammad, moved toward world domination. As Americans, the obvious question we should be asking ourselves is why, first of all, we allow the practice of this "religion" in our nation. Secondly, why do we allow its adherents to hold public office and pretend to be our "public servants"? Muslims are expressly forbidden to ally with a kafir (see 2. below) — so why would I expect my best interests to be represented by followers of Islam?

I have no problem with the *people* caught in the web of Islamic bondage; most Muslims are lovely human beings who have no idea what is in their holy books. Because it is a fear-based tyrannical system maintained by repression of knowledge and individual thought, few Muslims ever entertain the idea that they might investigate any other world view. Again, my problem is not with Muslims, it is with Islam itself.

Other religions outside the Judeo-Christian family which are practiced in America — for instance, Hinduism, Buddhism, and Hare Krishna — do not have an edict regarding my demise. Islam, however, refers to me, the "kafir", repeatedly in its law and the indication is that I do not deserve to live. This makes Islam my business.

Let's reiterate a few of the things we've looked at and apply them to our situation.

1. Why America is "Dar Al-Harb", or "The House of War" to Islam

"Muhammad: "I have been ordered to wage war against mankind until they accept that there is no god but Allah and that they believe I am His prophet and accept all revelations spoken through me. When they do these things I will protect their lives and property unless otherwise justified by Sharia, in which their fate lies in Allah's hands." **Sahih Muslim 001,0031.**

Since its founding, America has been a Christian nation, i.e., not under Sharia law. This makes us the "mankind" targeted here. These words of Muhammad are Islamic holy law.

I find it interesting that, in this statement of Muhammad it's almost as if he had read the end of the New Testament, learned that Jesus Christ will return to in fact set up His kingdom and reign over the entire earth (Revelation 19, 20, 21, 22), and decided to try and thwart it.

2. Why Muslim Congresswomen Make a Mockery of Our Government

No Muslim government official will ever consider — above Islamic law — any other law, nor the interests of Christians, Jews, Buddhists, Hindus, atheists, humanists, nor *any* outside Islam. They are forbidden by their law to be allied with us.

"The believers should not make the kafirs (all non-Muslims) their allies rather than other believers — anyone who does such a thing will isolate himself completely from God — except when you need to protect yourselves from them. God warns you to beware of Him; the Final Return is to God." **Qur'an 3:28.**

". . . they (kafirs) are your sworn enemies." **Qur'an 4:101.**

3. Why We Can Never, According to Islamic Law, Fully Believe that an Adherent to Islam Is Telling the Truth

Unfortunately, in Islam, there is a completely different standard for truth and honesty. According to Islamic law:

"Mohammad: 'A man who brings peace to the people by making up good words or by saying nice things, though untrue, does not lie.'" **Buhari 8,78,618.**

4. Why There Will Be Absolutely No Peace in the Middle East as Long as Islam Is in the Equation

If Muslims "talk" peace regarding any kafir nation, sadly, it doesn't mean anything:

"Believers! Obey Allah and the messenger, and do not let your effort be in vain. Those who do not believe and who prevent others from following Allah's path and then die as kafirs will not receive Allah's forgiveness. Therefore, do not be weak and offer the kafirs peace when you have the upper hand, for Allah is with you and will not begrudge you the reward of your deeds." Qur'an 47:33-35.

5. Why U.S. Citizens Must Wake Up to the Threat of Islam

A quote from a **1991 Muslim Brotherhood Document** which states instructions for the infiltration and establishment of Islamic power in North America:

> *"4- Understanding the role of the Muslim Brother in North America: The process of settlement is a "Civilization-Jihadist Process" with all the word means. The Ikhwan must understand that their work in America is a kind of grand Jihad in eliminating and destroying the Western civilization from within and "sabotaging" its miserable house by their hands and the hands of the believers so that it is eliminated and God's religion is made victorious over all other religions. Without this level of understanding, we are not up to this challenge and have not prepared ourselves for Jihad yet.*

It is a Muslim's destiny to perform Jihad and work wherever he is and wherever he lands until the final hour comes, and there is no escape from that destiny except for those who chose to slack. But, would the slackers and the Mujahedeen be equal."

This entire 1991 document drawn up by the Muslim Brotherhood can be found by visiting the site below. Once on the site, scroll down past the Arabic to the English.

http://www.investigativeproject.org/documents/misc/20.pdf

To see how this "grand Jihad" has already happened in Europe, watch a 2019 video produced by Katie Hopkins, called "Homeland" at:

https://www.youtube.com/watch?v=orTAUMMWd-A&t=9s.

Suggested Reading

Hatred's Kingdom
Dore Gold, Regnery Publishing, Inc. 2003

Islam Rising, Books 1, 2, 3
Dr. Jim Murk, 21st Century Press, 2007, 2009

Muslim Brotherhood: The Threat in our Backyard
Cathy Hinners, 2016

Rise in Defense of Judeo-Christian Values and Freedom
Brigitte Gabriel, Front Line, 2018

Sharia Law for Non-Muslims
Bill Warner, CSPI Publishing, 2010

Sword and Scimitar
Raymond Ibrahim, Da Capo Press, 2018

The Truth About Muhammad
Robert Spencer, Regnery Publishing, 2006

Thirteen Lessons on Political Islam, Islam 101
Bill Warner, CSPI Publishing, 2008

Important Cities of Early Islam

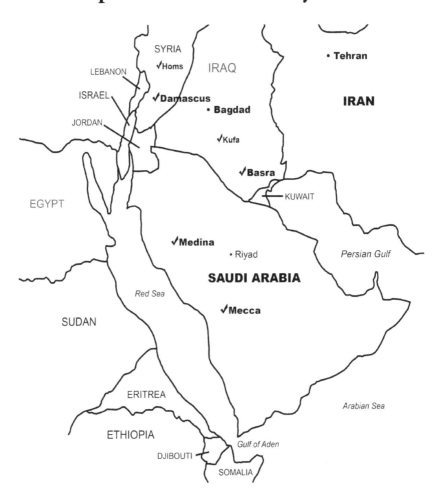

✔ Denotes cities that are referenced
within this book.

For more books and writings

or to contact Christina Bardstrum visit:

WWW.CHRISTINAFORTRUTH.COM

CPSIA information can be obtained
at www.ICGtesting.com
Printed in the USA
JSHW051835100820
7227JS00001B/43